CAN YOU GUESS
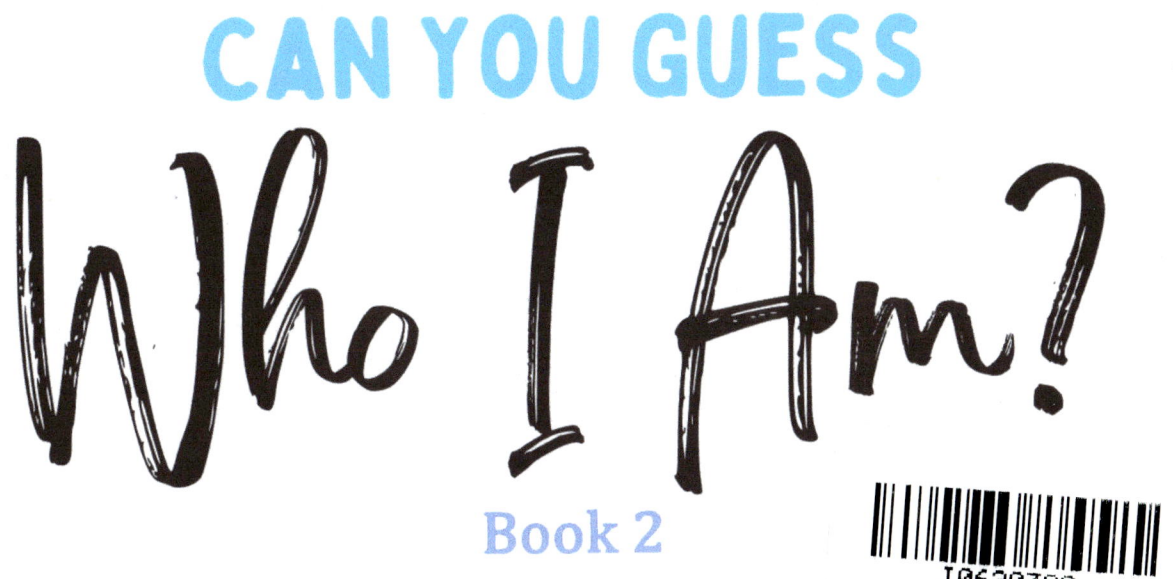
Who I Am?

Book 2

By Wayne McDonald
Illustrations by BJ McDonald

A concerted effort to present accurate details about the animals has been made. Information from places like zoos, aquariums and trusted online sources has been incorporated. Hopefully, you will give our efforts a passing grade.

Copyright 2025

Paperback ISBN: 978-1-953686-43-5
Hardcover ISBN: 978-1-953686-44-2
Library of Congress Control Number: 2024937084

WWW.LivingSpringsPublishers.com
Centennial, CO

Book design by Jacqueline Peavler.

Fish fishing by Vecteezy.com.
Jail by nelsonbro Vecteezy.com
Angler fish Image by Arhnue Tan from Pixabay

Acknowledgement

I wish to thank the following for helping me write my second book of animal riddle rhymes.

Ryan Herman and the staff at the **Downtown Aquarium** in Denver, CO, who graciously reviewed the poems in Book 2.

Marj McDonald, my wonderful wife, who puts up with a clicking keyboard late at night and early in the morning.

BJ McDonald, the artist who greatly enhances my books with her colorful pictures. My books are much better because of BJ.

Jordan McDonald, who helps me with everything associated with business and technology.

Kelsey Reynolds, the fantastic librarian who for some unknown reason continues to read everything I write – and has lived to tell about it. I could not do this without her guidance.

Kim Castor, the very supportive school librarian who encourages me and helps me find opportunities to read to more and more elementary students.

IT IS SO WONDERFUL TO HAVE FRIENDS AND FAMILY WHO BELIEVE IN AND SUPPORT YOUR WORK!

I dedicate my second book of
animal riddle rhymes to my very good friend

ALLEN BODENHAGEN.

A former elementary school teacher, he has now retired from
a long career as a human resource professional. His "loves"
include his wonderful wife (KaRene), his children and
grandchildren, hunting, fishing, boating, camping and reading.
A boy from western Pennsylvania, his professional journey has
taken him to Arkansas, Oklahoma, North Carolina and Georgia —
where I got to know and work with and for him. Allen is kind to
and respects everyone, and throughout his life has been a great
leader who worked diligently to grow and develop those on his
team. He was the best supervisor —and is the best friend — I
have ever had.

You are the detective!

Read the poems. They each have clues about an animal. Guess what the animal is before you turn the page.

Were you right?

Animals are amazing! Some interesting facts about each of the animals in the book are given to you; then we challenge you to find another fact.

Did you find the answer

DO YOU KNOW WHO WE ARE?

In tropical waters not many feet down
Some beautiful, colorful critters abound
They dig so neat into a coral reef
And live in a shiny "sea town"

Produces then releases a fluid out of its body.

To build, **secretes** fluid, no lumber to lug
Down there to the tunnel it dug
Forms tunnel wall with secretions, that's all
Home fits the worm nice and snug

Each worm, two trees, one color so bright
Not deep in the water so gets the sunlight
Sun makes'm shine in colors divine
Tis truly a diver's delight

They're orange and red and pink and white
And yellow and brown and blue and striped
You can see them all if your port of call
Takes you to a **Florida Key** site

Islands off the coast of Florida.

FLORIDA, USA

The "tree arms," so pretty, are helpful, too
They capture and then they funnel the food
So the worm can feed, take care of its needs.
Without these arms, what would worm do?

In order to breathe under water, needs gills
And this role the tree arms fulfill
So they are its feeder and also its breather
Do both jobs with wonderful skill

If preds come along, its trees do **retract**

Pulls back in.

In less than a second this worm does react
Cause crabs and fish surely do wish
To eat it for a mid-morning snack

A lifting door covering an opening.

Its home has a **trapdoor**, a special arm
That protects the worm from any alarm
When it does close, to a pred it does show
Spikes that could cause the pred harm

Doesn't stay closed very long, you see
Cause it can't eat with retracted trees
So peaks its trees out to serve as its scouts
If clear, they climb back out to feed
Tis a marvelous sea animal, indeed!
WHO ARE THESE SEA ANIMALS?

About the Christmas Tree Worm

This is a tiny, marine burrowing, segmented worm that lives in tropical waters around the world. It is about two inches long.

It has a well-developed nervous system and a central brain, plus a complete digestive system.

Each worm has two tree crowns. While the crowns can come in many colors, each worm shows the same color on both tree crowns.

The worm's "crowns" of tentacles are structures called radioles.

They dig a tunnel in live coral and then secrete a calcium carbonate (chalky) substance that forms the wall of their tunnel home.

They extend their tree-like crowns into the sea above their tunnels to breathe and feed. They live their lives in their tunnels, with only the "trees" above ground in the sea water.

When they sense danger, they retract their "trees" in milliseconds, down into their tunnel, and close their "trapdoor" with a special appendage that has spikes on the outside to ward off predators.

 **What are some other marine worms?**

DO YOU KNOW WHO I AM?

Don't make my own food, so an animal I am
Tentacles, food — into my mouth jams
And there's in me
Algae, you see
Feeds me and absorbs my debris

Pronounced "al-gee" - lives in animal's tissue.

That's good for me; I've just got a mouth
Don't have a "door" for poop to go out
And algae each day
Nice colors display
That you see through my clear arms' array

We both benefit.

Symbiotic, for me this works great
Algae lives safely inside my "estate"
Oxygen I get
Nutrients? You bet!
Algae gets carbon dioxide; no sweat!

I live attached — to the sea floor
No trip planner needed, for sure
In a colony I grow
Share food, you know
Thrive underwater but grow very slow -ly

6

NOW, LET'S TALK ABOUT A LARGE GROUP OF US!

Like beavers, we're builders and you value our worth
We built the biggest biological structures on Earth
Fourteen hundred miles, my man
Off Australia's Queensland
Is the length of the reef we have built in the sand

Millions of years this took to build
So we founded our very own **guild**
Successful we've been
But there is **chagrin**
For warming waters — threaten our "den"

A feeling of anger or disappointment.

If water's too hot, we lose our algae
Along with the colors you see in the sea
Bad for tourists like you
Bad for fisher folk, too
Who rely on the fish near our colony crew

Here's a clue for you: Reverse two letters and I'm a song you
might sing during the December holidays.

DO YOU KNOW OUR ANIMAL NAME?

About Coral

One coral is a polyp. A coral reef is built by and made up of thousands of coral polyps.

Coral polyps come in many sizes, with many being no wider than a nickel. A coral polyp is sort of like a tiny tin can, open at the top end, surrounded by a ring of tentacles that have stinging cells on them.

A coral is "sensile." This means it is permanently attached to the sea floor.

Shallow water corals get food via the stinging cells on their tentacles as well as from the algae that lives in their tissues. Deep water corals, without algae, must rely on their tentacles and stingers for food.

Algae provide green, brown and reddish colors to shallow water corals. Some of these corals make their own purple, blue or mauve colors.

Coral reefs are called the "rainforests of the sea" because about 25% of all ocean species depend on them for food and shelter.

 **What is the biggest coral reef in the world?**

DO YOU KNOW WHO I AM?

*This poem can be sung to the song titled
The Daring Young Man On The Flying Trapeze.*

I fly through the water with the greatest of ease
In oceans so deep that no human can see
I'm agile and speedy, from whales I do flee
Cause I want to live another day

Brain looks like a donut and this you can quote
Not made for dunking, but I sure can float
A head-footed critter, and others I **smote**
And m'throat does pass right through my brain

Strike or hit hard.

Eyes are **humongous**, and they're nicely spread
One "biggun" placed on each side of my head
Each filled with water; leaks out when I'm dead
And eyes collapse to a much smaller size

Really, really big!

I do have three hearts, now, just like my kin
One pumps blue blood from my head to my fins
While smaller hearts — take blood for a spin
To my gills found inside my torso

With arms on head and three hearts toward my rear
Not what you're used to, now that's very clear
A very strong jaw and a beak that can tear
Right through a wire made out of steel

Have two **appendages**, specially made
Shoot out to grab prey 'fore it can evade
These tentacles two — then make the trade
Hand prey to my eight waiting arms

Tis a sad story if you are the prey
Cause your time is over and you've gone away
But pred can be prey, so some do say
If pred is not always alert

Here now's the last clue, the last one you'll need
Tells how I survive way down here in the sea
I shoot out **black ink** when I need to flee
Shoot backwards just like a jet ski

WHO AM I?

About the Giant Squid

These "giants" can be up to 40 feet or so long (including the tentacles) and might weigh up to one ton. The mantle can be over six feet long.

Some of the reasons few humans have seen a live Giant Squid are:

They do not come to or near the surface to feed.

They live alone and do not congregate.

There is very little light in deep oceans, and the reddish coloring in their skin is not or almost not visible deep in the ocean.

The Giant Squid moves very fast and can change its skin color.

It is active at night when visibility is even lower down deep.

Humans would have to travel in very specialized equipment to get down to where giant squid live.

 **How big is the giant squid's eye?**

DO YOU KNOW WHO I AM?

I have a cousin, lives in oceans deep
She's scary as she can be
With a fishing rod and a light at the end
She fishes down in the deep sea

That doesn't seem fair!

Her rod is a fin that grows o'er her eyes
To out in front of her head
The rod has a light, shines so bright
And prey's lured right to the pred

When cuz opens mouth, you better watch out!
Mouth's full of sharp teeth and, surprise!
Her mouth and stomach both can **expand**
To swallow fish twice her size

Like a balloon.

BUT

Unlike my cuz, I don't live in the "deep"
I'm found — around — a coral reef
Don't have a light, but my lure's a sight!
Looks like a worm, I shake it, brings grief – to my prey

To hunt I wait patiently — on the sea floor
Waiting for "lunch" — and then I score
The great suction I cause as I rip open my jaws
Means prey's "history" forevermore

I can change my color there underwater
Just hang out, rest, and loiter
Yes, at **camo** I'm great down in my seascape
Helps me get lunch in short order

My color can match the ocean blue
ALERT! That is a **great clue** for you
Plus, I do look hairy, but do not be wary
For I am not poisonous to you

I walk on my fins; tis part of my fame
For I don't swim well in ocean "terrain"
Pectoral fins — have elbows that bend
And a "**croaker**" is part of my name

WHO IS THIS ANGLER FISH?

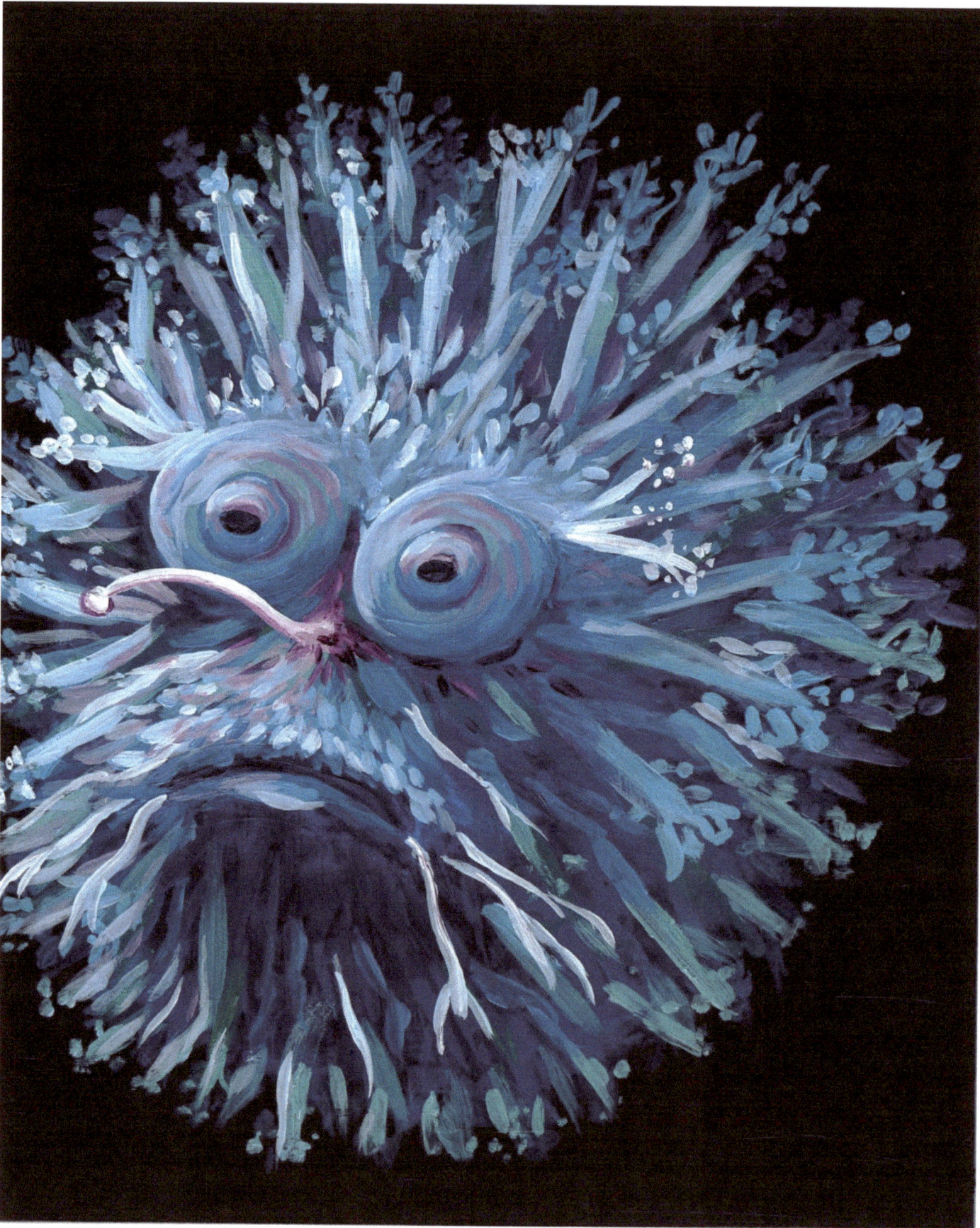

About the Hairy Frogfish

This shallow water angler fish lives in well-lit, surface waters in temperate and tropical regions.

It can change color to match its surroundings, but this takes days or weeks to accomplish.

Its four walking fins remind some of a frog, especially with the way its front fins bend forward.

It is covered in spinules that resemble hairs, hence the word "hairy" in its name.

There are over 200 species of angler fish and most live in the deep ocean. The angler fish portrayed in the *Finding Nemo* movie is a deep-sea angler fish.

Females produce a mass of eggs. The male then guards the eggs until they hatch.

 **How does the frogfish jump?**

DO YOU KNOW WHAT I AM?

I weigh 2 tons; quite heavy, you see
About 17 feet of me in the sea
I think I'm great, toot my own horn
In the ocean, you see, I'm a unicorn

I group with others, social they say
Like to hang out up in **Baffin Bay**
Being together is fun; but, brother!
Gotta be sure not to poke each other

Located between Canada and Greenland.

Things can go wrong for me, you see
Then you might find tusk pieces in me
Like an axolotl, I suck food right down
Down to my tummy where food is **ground**

My food is digested.

I come to the surface, have to breathe air
But sometimes the hole in the ice isn't there
A weather change quickly can lead to despair
And I have to hustle to find me some air

Tusk sensing temps can be my salvation
By helping me sense salt concentration
More salt means ice frozen, I cannot loiter
So I must flee to find open water — to breathe

Polar bears use — ice air holes as bait
Know I need air, so sit there and wait
Then some like me — do meet our fate
Sometimes you just can't escape

Our numbers, however, have not dropped
And I carry on, endangered I'm not!
Tusk looks like a horn, but doesn't blow
I carry it with me wherever I go

Like a fork!

I follow it as it leads the way
By 'bout 9 feet, it's ahead every day
It's my left canine that grew really long
Right one might grow to create a **prong**

WHAT AM I?

About the Narwhal

The narwhal is a whale, which is a mammal. Its name gets spelled three ways: narwal, narwhal and narwhale.

It has been called the "unicorn of the sea" because of its (usually) one horn, which is really the left canine tooth. It is a sensory organ with millions of nerve endings. Occasionally one will grow the right canine also.

Narwhals sometimes get tusk pieces stuck in their skin, but scientists do not know if this is by accident or from fighting.

They live in Arctic waters but are mostly found in Canada's Hudson Bay and Baffin Bay.

They change colors with age: blue-grey when born, blue-black as an adult, and almost white when old. They can dive 4,500 feet deep into the ocean.

 **How do Narwhal withstand incredible water pressure?**

DO YOU KNOW WHAT I AM?

I have a sharp beak but no bones, you see
An **invertebrate** is what you'd call me
Slippery I am
With no bones can
Change shape, escape and get free

> An animal without a backbone.

Could "ink" a contract, I'm very smart
My superpowers are off the charts
A limb I can lose
Don't get amused
But grow it back; don't need a Walmart

Jet propulsion for me is a cinch
It's something I only use in a pinch
Cause pressure on my mantle's
Almost more'n I can handle
Heart skips, and that makes me flinch

I get around other ways also
Can swim headfirst, crawl really slow
Some arms pull me
Others push, you see
But heart rate doubles, so far I don't go

To hunt, I drop — down onto prey
Snag'm with arms and beak makes my day
It sticks venom in
The prey and then
Prey becomes my delicious buffet
That I eat in a leisurely way – back in my den

I grab them, really fast.

One-third of my brain — is in my head
Two-thirds throughout my arms are spread
Arms can work, you see
Independently
Without input from head, tis said

I'm good at pretending to be something else.

A cephalopod, eight arms I've got
Master of disguise, I'm really hot!
Ink I can spread
To escape the pred
Can hide in the kelp, don't get caught

WHO AM I?

I'm not a squid!

23

About the Giant Pacific Octopus

This shy, reclusive, boneless invertebrate is the largest species of octopus in the world.

The adult has over 2,000 suction cups, in total, on its eight arms. This gives it a powerful grip.

It has toxic venom that is not fatal to humans if they are treated in a timely manner.

With jet propulsion and an ink spray that muddles the predator's senses, the giant Pacific octopus can escape in the blink of an eye.

It lives in the Pacific Ocean from Japan to Korea to Alaska and down to Baja California — in cold ocean waters.

The body of this octopus can be about two feet long. Its arms can span a distance of 13 feet or more.

To break open shelled animals (such as clams), it can pull the shell apart, bite it open with its beak, or drill a hole and inject venom into prey that is hard to open.

 **Is the giant Pacific octopus intelligent?**

DO YOU KNOW WHO I AM?

I'm an **apex predator**, the ocean's big dog
Humans come watch me; I leave'm agog
Weigh as much as an elephant
In the sea I am relevant
I really should have my own blog

At the top of the food chain.

I can be a pred of those moose, you see
Cause they swim tween islands off "**Alaskee**"
They have to look out
Cause if I'm about
I'm bigger, faster and on'm could feed

Alaska

The northernmost U.S. State.

Use **echolocation** down under the sea
Click sounds find prey, works well for me
A powerful jaw grip
And teeth that don't slip
Yep! Hunting for me is a breeze

Producing sound waves that echo off objects.

Some prey could harm me, so precautions I take
Toss'm in the air, grip'm and shake
Slap'm with tail
And ram'm quite well
Then tummy gets full as hunger I slake

Hold head above water to search for a seal
Resting on ice; then I reveal
My wave making skill
And that creature soon will
Fall in the ocean, become my next meal

I have been called the wolf of the sea
That's a name — that surely fits me
Give prey no slack
Hunt like a wolf pack
Meal options fit me to a "T"

They live in tight-knit family groups.

Strong **social structure**, like elephants and apes
And my comm skills are varied and great
Can teach my young
Things I have learned
To help'm thrive in our seascape

WHO AM I?

About the Orca

The orca is a dolphin, not a whale.

The basic orca group, a matriline, is headed up by the oldest female and can contain as many as four generations of family members. Several closely related matrilines can form a pod.

Orcas are found in all the world's oceans and in many seas. They generally prefer coastal areas at 60 to 90 degrees north or south of the Equator.

They are intelligent and live in complex, stable cultures among related groups that have no parallel except for humans.

Orcas communicate through a range of clicks, whistles, pulsed calls, squeals, squeaks and screams. They have distinct 'languages' within their family groups.

 **How do orcas sleep?**

DO YOU KNOW WHO I AM?

Down in deep waters I live — a sea slug
Look like a critter — you'd like to hug
A swimming snail, without a shell
But sea butterflies I do bug – because I eat'm

I look like an angel with two little wings
But up on my head sit horns, not rings
I don't have eyes; and that's a surprise
But my horns are my **sensory** things

I use them to sense things.

No central management system in me
Don't have a brain — researchers can see
Just **neuron** things that act like brains
One that's in each part of me

A neuron is a a single nerve cell.

My internal organs can really glow
And in orange and red and blue I go
Can glow in the deep, and that's really neat
Guess I like to put on a show

Eat other snails, I'm a carnivore
And I'm not a fish made with a light lure
But tentacles spread from inside my head
Grab prey and my lunch they secure

In the Antarctic, I ooze out a smell
A yucky odor that serves me quite well
Keeps preds away and that's okay
But sometimes I end up in **jail**!

Small sea animals with lots of legs.

Those **amphipods** are bigger than me
Have seven sets of legs, you see
With two legs, Jack, they trap me on their back
And it becomes curtains for me

What helps you can hurt, and here that's the case
Cause captured, I'm gone now, without a trace
My scent protects them, but for me it's grim
For my strength is no longer my ace

A lesson to be learned.

There is a **moral** to this story I'm told
For even if you are a predator bold
You shouldn't get cocky cause life can get rocky
And leave you out there in the cold.

WHO IS THIS "ANGEL WITH HORNS"?

About the Sea Angel

This invertebrate is called a sea angel because it exhibits a flying motion (like angels) when swimming. The wings have seven groups of muscles that move them.

It has six "thingys" (a new scientific term) that pop out of its head to capture prey. These are actually called Buccal cones. They conveniently surround the mouth.

This carnivore may look angelic, but it's not. With its tiny, toothed tongue, it rips or scrapes the prey from its shell (OUCH!) and cuts it into bits before it goes into the esophagus.

Some sit and wait for prey to meander by, while others actively pursue their food.

It glows in orange and red colors in the deep. It can also exhibit a blue color. There are over 3,000 species of sea angels.

The sea angel body is gelatinous and mostly transparent. Its snail "foot" evolved into two wings. It does NOT have a central brain but seems to manage without one just fine.

 **What is the difference between a sea angel and a sea butterfly?**

DO YOU KNOW WHO I AM?

An ambush pred, I'm a good scout
Skin texture blends, gives me fishing clout
And get this, my brother
My skin can change color
And I suck food right into my snout

My **digestive system's** unique
And constantly I have to eat
Brine shrimp, they say
Three thousand a day
So that I can my food needs meet

Body parts that help me digest food.

One eye moves left while other moves right
For hunting pred, gives me great sight
And a body I bring
Of camo styled rings
Catch prey before they can take flight

The **Triple Crown** I'll never win
Swim upright, fast never been
Just a slow fish
How I do wish
I had me a big dorsal fin

Awarded to the rare winner of 3 big horse races.

Emperor penguin dad is no slouch
Keeps his egg warm for months, no doubt
Yet I have it rough
Cause female does stuff
Thousands of eggs in my **pouch!**

A kangaroo
has a pouch
too.

I bulk up as my babies grow
Take'm with me wherever I go
But when the time comes
For them to move on
I eject'm and that's quite a show!

My head and neck look like a horse
Prehensile tail keeps me on course
It wraps around the
Seaweed way down
To keep me near my food source
WHO AM I?

Can grasp
or hold
objects.

About the Seahorse

Seahorses live in warm, salty waters (near coral reefs, seagrass, and mangrove trees) in the Atlantic and Pacific Oceans, in the Mediterranean Sea, and other places.

Sometimes, storms at sea overpower its ability to hold on with its tail, and it gets swept far away – from its mate and from its food source.

It does not look like a fish, but it is one. It comes with a swim bladder to give it buoyancy.

For a fish, it is unique in that it can move forward, backward, up, and down – just not very fast.

The largest seahorse species is the size of a banana. The smallest seahorse is only half an inch long (13 mm)!

Most wild seahorses only have one partner during their life.

Soon after one batch is born, the female presents the male with another batch of eggs. Do you think the seahorse should be the father of the year?

 **Does a seahorse make noise?**

DO YOU KNOW WHO ARE WE?

Think of some strings that you could take
And tie them in knots until you did make
It long, what a feat
Over one hundred fifty feet
Until you DID NEED A BREAK!

I recently read of a critter like this
That lives in the oceans' deep **abyss**
Looks like a string
But really can sting
Fish get gobbled if they are careless

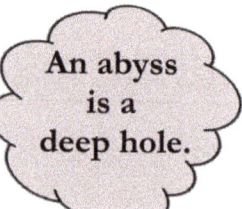

An abyss is a deep hole.

This sea life so long, that's just a mask
It's thousands together as prey does swim past
United as one
To get the job done
Each "**string part**" has its own task

This animal is a colony of individual parts, called "zooids"

Some make more parts, that's their station
Some help catch food, that's their donation
Others digest
Tis what they do best
While others control its flotation.

These tiny critters become deadly foes
For tiny sea life that's caught in its **throes**
One? Not a "prob"
But in thousands, they rob
Their prey of its life down below

These things so like jelly deep down in the sea
With **no bones** in'm, they're amazing to me
How did they adapt
To close the size gap
And become such a threat in the deep?

But a good lesson learned is how they've survived
By joining in thousands they have surprised
Much bigger threats
And they are here yet
And get to live out their own lives

WHO ARE THEY?

About the Siphonophore

Yes, some (not all) do look like strings in the water. Look it up yourself!

These carnivores sting and stun their prey (small fish, crustaceans) before killing and eating them.

Thousands of these individuals can live together in a "colony string," appearing to be one sea creature. Such a colony, collectively, may be the longest animal in the world.

What they accomplish together far exceeds what each one could do as an individual. That's a great lesson!

Some of them emit bioluminescent light (green, blue, or red) to attract prey. This light apparently keeps the prey from identifying the predator.

The larger/longer siphonophores live in deeper waters in all oceans, so you'll probably never meet one.

They have tentacles used to catch prey. Each tentacle is equipped with a stinging capability

 **What animals prey on siphonophores?**

Do You Recognize Me Now?

About the Author

 Wayne McDonald is a graduate of the University of North Carolina, Chapel Hill, NC, where he obtained a Bachelor of Arts degree in Elementary Education and a Master of Education degree in Education Administration. While there, he completed the U.S. Air Force ROTC program with distinction and was designated an Outstanding Graduate. He retired in the Denver, CO, area after an Air Force career that took him to Europe, Asia and multiple places in the U.S. He retired with the rank of Colonel. He is the recipient of multiple medals including the Legion of Merit. He has worked for Littleton Public Schools, Littleton, CO, and is currently serving as a Senior Volunteer, reading animal poems to elementary students. He also works for the First Tee Colorado Mountains and for the South Suburban Parks and Recreation District. Once a week or so, he reaffirms his status as a certified duffer at the South Suburban Golf Course in Centennial.

About the Illustrator

BJ McDonald, M.Ed. is a professional artist and educational specialist with over two decades of experience working with children. She channels both her artistic talents and her understanding of children's literature into her work. A self-taught artist, BJ has crafted her own unique style of vibrant, acrylic paintings over the years, drawing from her travels to paint compelling scenery. Her work, including her murals, can be found around the Denver Metro area. Outside of teaching and painting, BJ is a proud mother and a volunteer for the International Dyslexia Association-Rocky Mountain Branch.

www.bettyejean.com

@bettyejeanart

GUESS WHAT'S COMING!

"Who Am I Book 3"

We are already working on the next book in the series. It will have poems about more fascinating animals.

Visit LivingspringsPublishers.com and sign up for our newsletter to be notified when it is released.

You can also find links to online stores where our books can be purchased on our website.

What are some other marine worms?

Polychaete are a group of segmented worms that contains over 13,000 species. Some of the strangest creatures on our planet are worms. The marine worm; feather duster worm; lugworm; and the clam worm are just a few.

What is the biggest coral reef in the world?

The Great Barrier Reef is the world's largest coral reef system. It has 2,900 individual reefs and 900 islands stretching for over 1,400 miles. It is in the Coral Sea, off the coast of Queensland, Australia. It can be seen from outer space and is the world's biggest single structure made by living organisms.

How big is the giant squid's eye?

Giant squid, along with their cousin, the colossal squid, have beach-ball size eyes! Their eyes are the largest eyes in the animal kingdom and are about 10 inches in diameter.

How does the frogfish jump?

Frogfish really are jet propelled! They jump by sucking water in through the mouth and expelling it through the small gill openings behind their "legs".

How do Narwhal withstand incredible water pressure?

Narwhal can dive a mile deep and stay underwater for over 25 minutes before having to surface for air. They have compressible rib cages which can be squeezed without harming them when swimming at huge depths.

Is the giant Pacific octopus intelligent?

The giant Pacific octopus can learn to open jars, interact with caretakers, and squeeze through very small spaces.

How do orcas sleep?

Orcas need to remember to breathe, even when they are sleeping! So, one half of the brain rests while the other half stays alert to control breathing, consequently keeping one eye open! This is a form of sleep known as unihemispheric sleep.

What is the difference between a sea angel and a sea butterfly?

They are both pteropods — swimming sea snails and slugs. Sea angels, or Gymnosomata (which means "naked body"), do not have a shell. Sea butterflies (Thecosomata) are usually smaller and have shells. Sea angels' prey on sea butterflies.

Does a seahorse make noise?

Seahorses make noise! They make noises that can be heard underwater similar to the sound of smacking your lips. They make the noise during feeding and courtship.

What animals prey on siphonophores?

Some animals, like leatherback sea turtles and large fish, eat siphonophores. Pram bugs, which are deep sea crustaceans, chew their way into siphonophores to live inside them, often killing them in the process. Generally, a siphonophore's stinging tentacles keep it protected from predators.

www.ingramcontent.com/pod-product-compliance
Lightning Source LLC
Chambersburg PA
CBHW041126120626
46547CB00019B/2874